Table of Cotents

Introduction

Balance Exercises for Seniors

10-Minute Daily Routines to Enhance Stability and Prevent Falls. A 4-Week Illustrated Fitness Guide to Regaining Confidence and Mobility at Home

Copyright Notice:

Disclaimer:

The information provided in this document is for general informational purposes only. All content is provided in good faith; however, we make no representations or warranties of any kind, express or implied, regarding the accuracy, adequacy, validity, reliability, availability, or completeness of the information in this document. Under no circumstances shall we be liable for any loss or damage of any kind incurred as a result of using this document or relying on the information provided. Your use of this document and any reliance on its contents is solely at your own risk.

Introduction

Why Balance Matters for Seniors

As we age, the significance of maintaining balance becomes increasingly apparent. For seniors, balance is not merely about avoiding falls; it's a fundamental aspect of preserving independence and ensuring a high quality of life. Understanding why balance is so crucial and how it impacts daily living can help motivate seniors to prioritize this critical aspect of their health.

The Impact of Aging on Balance

Aging brings about a range of physical and neurological changes that can affect balance. Muscle mass and strength often decrease, joints may become stiffer, and the sensory systems—such as vision, proprioception (the sense of body position), and the vestibular system (inner ear balance mechanisms)—can deteriorate. These changes collectively contribute to a decline in balance, making everyday tasks more challenging.

For many seniors, this decline can manifest in difficulties with walking, standing up from a seated position, or even reaching for an object. As these tasks become harder, the risk of falls increases significantly. Falls are not just a minor inconvenience; they can lead to severe injuries such as fractures or head trauma, which can have lasting impacts on health and mobility.

The Risk of Falls

Falls are a leading cause of injury among seniors and can have serious consequences. According to the Centers for Disease Control and Prevention (CDC), one in four older adults falls each year, and falls are the leading cause of both fatal and non-fatal injuries in this age group. The impact of a fall can be devastating, leading to fractures, head injuries, and a reduced ability to move freely. Beyond physical injuries, falls can instill a fear of falling, which may cause seniors to limit their activities. This reduced activity can further weaken muscles and decrease balance, creating a dangerous cycle.

Preserving Independence Through Balance

Maintaining good balance is crucial for performing daily activities safely and independently. Balance affects the ability to walk steadily, stand without support, and navigate environments confidently. For seniors, the ability to move around their home and community with ease is essential for independence. Effective balance exercises can help counteract the effects of aging by strengthening muscles, improving coordination, and enhancing sensory feedback, all of which contribute to better stability and reduced fall risk.

Balance exercises also play a role in improving functional abilities such as getting in and out of a car, climbing stairs, or bending down to pick something up. These are key activities that support daily living and overall quality of life. By enhancing balance, seniors can maintain their ability to perform these activities with greater ease and confidence.

Balance and Overall Well-Being

The benefits of balance exercises extend beyond fall prevention. Regular balance training can lead to improvements in overall physical health, including increased muscle strength, flexibility, and joint mobility. Additionally, engaging in balance exercises has been shown to improve mood and reduce symptoms of depression and anxiety, contributing to a more positive outlook on life.

Balance exercises often involve gentle movements that can help reduce chronic pain and stiffness, making them a valuable addition to a comprehensive health regimen. The increased sense of control over one's body and environment can enhance self-esteem and foster a more active and fulfilling lifestyle.

A Call to Action

For seniors, prioritizing balance is not just about physical health but about maintaining a high quality of life. By understanding the impact of aging on balance and taking proactive steps to address it, seniors can significantly reduce their risk of falls, preserve their independence, and enjoy a more active and fulfilling life. Embracing balance exercises as a regular part of your routine can make a profound difference in how you feel and function every day.

Investing in balance and stability today will pay dividends in the form of enhanced safety, confidence, and overall well-being in the future. Balance is not just a physical attribute but a cornerstone of a vibrant and independent life.

Getting Started

What You Need: Space, Equipment, and Mindset

Before embarking on this program, it's important to prepare your environment and mindset.

- Space: Ensure you have a clear, open space where you can move freely. This area should be free of obstacles and provide enough room to perform exercises safely.

- Equipment: While many exercises require no equipment, having a few basic items can enhance your workout. Consider a sturdy chair for support, a yoga mat for comfort, and light weights or resistance bands if appropriate.

- Mindset: Approach the program with a positive and committed attitude. Consistency is key to achieving results, and maintaining motivation is crucial for long-term success.

How to Use This 4-Week Program

The 4-week program outlined in this book is structured to progressively build your balance and stability. Each week introduces new exercises that build on previous ones, helping you gradually improve your skills and confidence. The program includes daily 10-minute routines designed to fit easily into your schedule. To get the most out of the program, follow the instructions carefully, use the provided illustrations, and keep track of your progress through the reflection sections at the end of each week.

The book is structured to guide you through the process, offering support and adjustments as needed. By adhering to the program and incorporating the exercises into your routine, you will foster improved balance, mobility, and overall well-being.

Chapter 1: Understanding Balance and Stability

- How Balance Works

    The Role of Muscles, Joints, and the Nervous System

- Challenges of Aging

    Common Causes of Balance Decline and Falls

- Benefits of Balance Exercises

    Improving Stability, Mobility, and Confidence

How Balance Works

How Balance Works: The Role of Muscles, Joints, and the Nervous System

Introduction

Balance is fundamental to all human movement, from the simplest act of standing still to the most complex athletic feats. It allows us to maintain stability, coordinate our movements, and interact safely with our environment. The process of balancing involves a sophisticated interplay between muscles, joints, and the nervous system, all working in concert to keep us upright and oriented. Understanding this intricate system can provide insights into maintaining balance and preventing falls, particularly as we age or recover from injury.

The Role of Muscles

Muscles are the body's primary actuators, responsible for generating the forces that control movement and stability. They are essential for maintaining balance, both in static postures and dynamic movements.

1. Postural Muscles:

   - Core Musculature: The muscles of the abdomen, lower back, and pelvis, collectively known as the core, are particularly crucial for balance. These muscles stabilize the spine and pelvis, providing a solid foundation for all movements. A strong core reduces the risk of falls by improving overall stability.

   - Leg Muscles: The muscles in the legs, especially the quadriceps, hamstrings, and calf muscles, are key players in maintaining balance. They provide the necessary strength to support the body's weight and adjust the center of gravity during movement.

   - Neck and Shoulder Muscles: These muscles help maintain head position and upper body posture, which are essential for balance, especially when visual cues are important.

2. Anticipatory Muscle Activity:

   - Coordination: Before any voluntary movement, such as lifting an arm or stepping forward, muscles throughout the body engage in anticipatory postural adjustments (APAs). This coordinated muscle activity stabilizes the body in preparation for the movement, ensuring that balance is maintained.

   - Preventing Instability: APAs are critical for preventing instability during complex tasks, such as reaching for an object while standing on one leg. They involve the pre-activation of muscles that counterbalance the expected shift in the center of gravity.

3. Reflexive Muscle Responses:

   - Rapid Corrections: When balance is unexpectedly disturbed, such as when slipping on ice, the body relies on reflexive muscle contractions to quickly restore stability. These reflexes are automatic and involve the rapid activation of muscles in the legs, core, and arms.

   - Stretch Reflex: A key component of reflexive muscle responses is the stretch reflex, which is triggered when a muscle is suddenly stretched. This reflex causes the muscle to contract quickly, helping to prevent a fall by rapidly correcting the body's position.

The Role of Joints

Joints, the connections between bones, provide the flexibility and movement necessary for maintaining balance. They allow the body to make the fine adjustments required to keep the center of gravity over the base of support.

1. Joint Proprioception:

   - Sensory Feedback: Joints contain proprioceptors—specialized sensors that provide continuous feedback to the brain about joint position and movement. This feedback is crucial for adjusting muscle activity and maintaining balance, especially during dynamic activities like walking or running.

   - Ankle and Knee Joints: The ankle and knee joints are particularly important for balance. The ankle joint, in particular, allows for subtle adjustments that keep the body stable on uneven surfaces. The knee joint contributes by absorbing shocks and providing the necessary support during weight-bearing activities.

2. Range of Motion:

   - Flexibility and Balance: The range of motion at a joint determines how well the body can adapt to different balance challenges. For instance, the ability to flex and extend the ankle joint is crucial for maintaining balance on inclines or during sudden directional changes.

   - Impact of Limited Mobility: Reduced range of motion, whether due to stiffness, injury, or age, can impair balance. For example, limited ankle mobility can prevent effective balance corrections, increasing the risk of falls.

3. Joint Stability:

   - Structural Integrity: Joint stability is provided by the ligaments, tendons, and muscles that surround and support the joint. Stable joints are less likely to move excessively, which is important for maintaining balance during dynamic movements.

   - Balance Training: Exercises that enhance joint stability, such as balance training on unstable surfaces, can improve overall balance by strengthening the muscles and ligaments around key joints like the ankle and knee.

The Role of the Nervous System

The nervous system is the control center for balance, orchestrating the complex interplay between sensory input, motor output, and cognitive processing to maintain stability.

1. Sensory Input:

   - The Vestibular System: Located in the inner ear, the vestibular system detects changes in head position and motion, providing critical information about balance and spatial orientation. It helps the brain understand the body's position relative to gravity and movement.

   - Visual System: Vision plays a significant role in balance by providing the brain with information about the environment, such as the position of objects, surfaces, and potential obstacles. Visual input is especially important when navigating complex environments or when other sensory inputs are compromised.

   - Somatosensory System: This system includes proprioceptors in the muscles, tendons, and skin that detect the position and movement of the body. It allows the nervous system to make precise adjustments to muscle activity, helping to maintain balance even in challenging conditions.

2. Central Processing:

   - Cerebellum: The cerebellum, located at the back of the brain, is the primary center for coordinating balance. It integrates sensory information from the vestibular system, visual system, and proprioceptors to fine-tune muscle activity and maintain stability.

   - Brainstem: The brainstem manages automatic balance responses, such as reflexive muscle contractions. It plays a key role in the body's rapid, involuntary reactions to balance disturbances, such as stumbling or tripping.

3. Motor Output:

   - Coordination of Movements: Once the brain processes sensory input, it sends signals to the muscles to execute the necessary movements to maintain balance. This coordination involves both voluntary movements, such as stepping or turning, and involuntary adjustments, such as reflexive muscle contractions.

   - Feedback Loops: The nervous system continuously monitors and adjusts muscle activity based on feedback from the sensory systems. This feedback loop allows for constant fine-tuning of balance, ensuring that the body can adapt to changing conditions in real time.

The Impact of External Factors on Balance

1. Environmental Challenges:

   - Surface Conditions: Walking on uneven, slippery, or unstable surfaces requires the body to make constant adjustments to maintain balance. The nervous system must quickly process sensory input and adjust muscle activity to prevent falls.

   - Visual Distractions: Poor lighting, visual clutter, or sudden changes in the environment can disrupt the visual system's ability to provide accurate information to the brain, making it harder to maintain balance.

2. Footwear and Equipment:

   - Shoes: The type of footwear can significantly impact balance. Shoes that provide good support and a stable base can enhance balance, while those with high heels or slippery soles can increase the risk of falls.

   - Assistive Devices: For individuals with impaired balance, assistive devices such as canes, walkers, or balance braces can help stabilize the body and reduce the risk of falls.

3. Physical and Mental Fatigue:

   - Muscle Fatigue: When muscles are fatigued, their ability to respond quickly and effectively to balance challenges is compromised. This increases the risk of falls, particularly during prolonged physical activity.

   - Cognitive Load: Balance also requires cognitive resources, particularly in complex or challenging environments. When the brain is overloaded with tasks, such as multitasking while walking, balance can be compromised.

How Balance Deteriorates

1. Aging:

   - Muscle Atrophy: As we age, muscle mass and strength tend to decrease, which can impair the ability to maintain balance. This muscle atrophy is often accompanied by a decline in the effectiveness of anticipatory and reflexive muscle responses.

   - Joint Stiffness: Aging often leads to reduced joint flexibility, particularly in the ankles and knees. This stiffness can limit the range of motion and reduce the ability to make the fine adjustments needed for balance.

   - Sensory Decline: The sensory systems that contribute to balance, including vision, proprioception, and the vestibular system, often become less effective with age. This decline can lead to slower and less accurate balance corrections.

2. Injury:

- Musculoskeletal Injuries: Injuries to muscles, ligaments, or joints can disrupt the balance system. For example, a sprained ankle can impair proprioception and joint stability, leading to increased instability and a higher risk of future falls.

- Neurological Injuries: Injuries to the brain or spinal cord can impair the nervous system's ability to process sensory information and coordinate motor responses. This can result in significant balance problems, requiring rehabilitation and adaptive strategies.

3. Neurological Conditions:

- Parkinson's Disease: This progressive neurological disorder affects movement and balance, leading to symptoms such as tremors, stiffness, and impaired coordination. Balance problems are common in Parkinson's disease, making falls a major concern.

- Multiple Sclerosis (MS): MS is a disease that affects the central nervous system, leading to a wide range of symptoms, including balance issues. The disease can cause muscle weakness, coordination problems, and sensory disturbances, all of which can impair balance.

- Stroke: A stroke can damage the areas of the brain responsible for processing sensory information and coordinating muscle activity. Depending on the severity and location of the stroke, this can lead to significant balance impairments.

Strategies to Improve and Maintain Balance

1. Exercise and Physical Therapy:

- Strength Training: Strengthening the muscles that support balance, particularly the core and lower body muscles, can significantly improve stability. Exercises such as squats, lunges, and leg raises are particularly effective.

- Balance Exercises: Specific balance exercises, such as standing on one leg, using a balance board, or practicing yoga, can improve proprioception, joint stability, and overall balance.

- Flexibility Training: Stretching exercises that improve the range of motion in the joints, particularly the ankles and hips, can enhance balance by allowing for greater movement flexibility and more effective balance corrections.

2. Cognitive Training:

- Dual-Task Training: Training that involves performing cognitive tasks while maintaining balance can improve the brain's ability to manage multiple demands simultaneously, which is particularly useful for preventing falls in complex environments.

- Mindfulness and Focus: Techniques that enhance awareness and focus, such as mindfulness meditation, can improve the ability to maintain balance by reducing distractions and enhancing concentration on the body's movements.

3. Lifestyle Adjustments:

- Healthy Diet: A diet rich in nutrients, particularly those that support muscle and bone health, such as calcium, vitamin D, and protein, can help maintain muscle strength and joint health, both of which are crucial for balance.

- Proper Footwear: Wearing shoes that provide good support and a stable base can enhance balance, particularly for older adults or those with balance impairments.

- Environmental Modifications: making changes to the home environment, such as installing handrails, removing tripping hazards, and improving lighting, can reduce the risk of falls and enhance balance.

Conclusion

Balance is a complex, dynamic process that involves the coordinated efforts of muscles, joints, and the nervous system. Each of these components plays a critical role in maintaining stability and preventing falls, particularly in challenging or changing environments. As we age or recover from injury, understanding how balance works can help us take proactive steps to preserve it, such as engaging in targeted exercises, making lifestyle adjustments, and seeking appropriate medical care. By maintaining and improving balance, we can continue to move confidently and safely, enjoying an active and independent life.

Challenges of Aging

Introduction

Aging brings about a host of changes in the body, many of which can impact balance and increase the risk of falls. Falls are a leading cause of injury among older adults and can lead to serious consequences, including fractures, loss of independence, and even death. Understanding the common causes of balance decline and falls is crucial for preventing these incidents and promoting healthy aging.

Physical Changes

Affecting Balance

As we age, several physical changes occur that can compromise our ability to maintain balance and increase the likelihood of falls.

1.   Muscle Weakness:

Sarcopenia: Aging is often accompanied by sarcopenia, the gradual loss of muscle mass and strength. This decline typically begins around the age of 30 and accelerates after 60. Weaker muscles mean less stability and a reduced ability to correct balance when it is disturbed.

Impact on Posture: Muscle weakness can also lead to poor posture, such as forward head posture or stooped shoulders, which shifts the center of gravity and makes balance more challenging.

2.   Joint Stiffness and Reduced Flexibility:

Arthritis: Conditions like osteoarthritis are common with aging and can cause joint pain, stiffness, and swelling. These symptoms reduce the range of motion, making it difficult to perform balance corrections or move fluidly, particularly in the ankles, knees, and hips.

Decreased Mobility: Stiff joints and reduced flexibility limit the body's ability to adapt to changes in the environment, such as stepping over obstacles or adjusting to uneven surfaces, which increases the risk of falls.

3. Decline in Sensory Systems:

Vision: Age-related changes in vision, such as cataracts, glaucoma, or macular degeneration, reduce the ability to see clearly, especially in low-light or high-contrast environments. Vision is a key component of balance, and any impairment can make it difficult to judge distances, see obstacles, or detect changes in terrain.

Vestibular System: The vestibular system, located in the inner ear, helps control balance by detecting changes in head position and movement. With age, this system can become less effective, leading to dizziness, vertigo, and an increased risk of falls.

Proprioception: Proprioception is the body's ability to sense its position in space, and it relies on feedback from joints, muscles, and skin. As we age, the sensitivity of proprioceptors decreases, making it harder to detect changes in body position and respond quickly to maintain balance.

Health Conditions Contributing to Balance Decline

Several health conditions that become more common with age can also contribute to balance decline and increase the risk of falls.

1. Neurological Disorders:

Parkinson's Disease: Parkinson's disease affects movement and balance, leading to symptoms such as tremors, stiffness, and slow movements. These symptoms can make it difficult to maintain balance, particularly when walking or changing direction.

Stroke: A stroke can cause damage to the brain that affects balance and coordination. Depending on the severity and location of the stroke, this can result in weakness, paralysis, or impaired proprioception, all of which increase the risk of falls.

Peripheral Neuropathy: This condition, often associated with diabetes, involves damage to the nerves in the extremities, particularly the feet. It can lead to numbness, tingling, and loss of sensation, making it difficult to detect changes in surface texture or maintain balance.

2. Cardiovascular Issues:

Low Blood Pressure (Hypotension): Orthostatic hypotension, a sudden drop in blood pressure when standing up, is common in older adults. It can cause dizziness, lightheadedness, and even fainting, increasing the risk of falls.

Heart Disease: Conditions such as arrhythmias or congestive heart failure can lead to dizziness, fatigue, and reduced stamina, making it harder to maintain balance and increasing the likelihood of falls.

3.   Cognitive Decline:

Dementia: Cognitive impairments associated with dementia can affect the ability to process sensory information and make decisions quickly. Individuals with dementia may also have difficulty remembering to use assistive devices, navigate their environment safely, or recognize hazards, all of which contribute to an increased risk of falls.

Slower Reaction Times: Aging often results in slower cognitive processing and reaction times, making it harder to respond quickly to balance challenges, such as tripping over an object or navigating a crowded space.

Environmental Factors

The physical environment plays a significant role in fall risk, particularly for older adults who may already be dealing with balance issues.

1.   Hazards at Home:

Clutter and Obstacles: Clutter, loose rugs, and electrical cords can create tripping hazards in the home. Navigating around furniture or stepping over obstacles becomes more challenging with age-related balance decline.

Poor Lighting: Inadequate lighting in the home, particularly at night, can make it difficult to see potential hazards. This is particularly dangerous for older adults with impaired vision or slower reaction times.

2.	Unsafe Footwear:

Improper Shoes: Wearing shoes that do not fit properly, have slippery soles or lack support can significantly increase the risk of falls. High heels, sandals, and shoes without backs are particularly hazardous for older adults.

Walking Barefoot: While comfortable, walking barefoot or in socks on slippery surfaces like hardwood or tile floors can increase the risk of slips and falls.

3.	Outdoor Hazards:

Uneven Surfaces: Uneven sidewalks, cracks in pavement, and loose gravel are common outdoor hazards that can trip up even those with good balance. These hazards are particularly dangerous for older adults with reduced proprioception or joint flexibility.

Weather Conditions: Rain, ice, and snow can create slippery surfaces that are challenging to navigate. Cold weather can also stiffen joints and slow reaction times, further increasing the risk of falls.

Medication and Balance

Many older adults take medications that can affect balance, either directly or through side effects.

1.	Side Effects of Medications:

Dizziness and Drowsiness: Some medications, particularly sedatives, antihypertensives, and certain antidepressants, can cause dizziness or drowsiness, making it harder to maintain balance. The risk is higher when multiple medications with these side effects are taken together, a situation known as polypharmacy.

Balance Impairment: Medications that affect the central nervous system, such as benzodiazepines or anticholinergics, can impair coordination and balance, leading to an increased risk of falls.

2.   Interactions and Polypharmacy:

Cumulative Effects: As people age, they are more likely to be prescribed multiple medications. The combined effects of these drugs can lead to increased dizziness, fatigue, and confusion, all of which impair balance and increase fall risk.

Monitoring and Adjustment: Regular review of medications by healthcare providers is essential for minimizing the risk of falls. Adjusting dosages, switching medications, or eliminating unnecessary drugs can help reduce side effects that impact balance.

Psychological and Behavioral Factors

Psychological and behavioral factors can also contribute to balance decline and fall risk in older adults.

1.   Fear of Falling:

Cycle of Fear and Inactivity: The fear of falling can lead to reduced physical activity, which in turn weakens muscles and further impairs balance. This creates a vicious cycle where fear leads to increased fall risk due to decreased physical fitness and confidence.

Overcompensation: Some older adults may overcompensate for their fear by walking more slowly or rigidly, which can actually increase the risk of falls by making movements less fluid and more awkward.

2.   Depression and Anxiety:

Impact on Balance: Depression and anxiety can lead to decreased energy, concentration, and motivation, all of which can affect balance. These conditions are also associated with slower reaction times and reduced physical activity, further increasing fall risk.

Medication Side Effects: The medications used to treat depression and anxiety, such as antidepressants or anxiolytics, can have side effects that impair balance, such as dizziness, drowsiness, or coordination issues.

3.   Risk-Taking Behaviors:

Overconfidence: Some older adults may underestimate their risk of falling and engage in behaviors that increase fall risk, such as climbing ladders, rushing, or carrying heavy objects without assistance.

Ignoring Precautions: Failing to use assistive devices like canes or walkers, neglecting to wear proper footwear, or not paying attention to environmental hazards can all contribute to an increased risk of falls.

Preventing Balance Decline and Falls

While aging naturally brings about changes that can affect balance, there are proactive steps that can be taken to reduce the risk of falls and maintain independence.

1.   Regular Exercise:

Strength and Balance Training: Engaging in regular exercise that focuses on strength, balance, and flexibility can help counteract the effects of aging on muscles and joints. Tai Chi, yoga, and specific balance exercises are particularly effective.

Aerobic Activity: Walking, swimming, or cycling can improve cardiovascular health, endurance, and overall physical fitness, all of which contribute to better balance and reduced fall risk.

2.   Home Modifications:

Removing Hazards: Clearing clutter, securing loose rugs, and ensuring that electrical cords are out of the way can reduce the risk of trips and falls. Installing grab bars in the bathroom, adding railings to stairs, and improving lighting throughout the home are also effective strategies to make the home environment safer and reduce fall risks.

3. Proper Footwear:

 - Choosing Supportive Shoes: Wearing shoes that fit well, have non-slip soles, and provide adequate support can greatly reduce the risk of falls. Avoiding high heels, loose slippers, or shoes without backs is important for maintaining stability.

 - Using Orthotics: For individuals with foot problems, custom orthotics can help correct alignment issues and improve balance, further reducing fall risk.

4. Medication Management:

  - Regular Reviews: Regularly reviewing medications with a healthcare provider can help identify and mitigate any drugs that may contribute to balance problems. This might involve adjusting dosages, switching to alternatives with fewer side effects, or discontinuing unnecessary medications.

  - Awareness of Side Effects: Being aware of potential side effects, such as dizziness or drowsiness, and taking precautions, such as rising slowly from a seated position, can help reduce the risk of falls related to medication use.

5. Vision and Hearing Care:

  - Regular Check-Ups: Regular eye and ear exams can help detect and correct issues that might impair balance. Wearing appropriate glasses, contact lenses, or hearing aids can improve sensory input, making it easier to navigate the environment safely.

  - Environmental Adjustments: Ensuring good lighting, reducing glare, and minimizing visual clutter in the home can also help compensate for age-related vision changes.

6. Use of Assistive Devices:

  - Canes and Walkers: Using assistive devices like canes, walkers, or rollators can provide additional support and stability, particularly for individuals with significant balance challenges. It's important to use these devices properly and ensure they are adjusted to the correct height.

  - Mobility Aids: For those with more severe balance issues, mobility aids such as wheelchairs or scooters can help maintain independence while reducing the risk of falls.

7. Fall Prevention Programs:

  - Community Programs: Many communities offer fall prevention programs specifically designed for older adults. These programs often include exercises to improve strength and balance, education on fall prevention strategies, and assessments to identify personal risk factors.

  - Occupational Therapy: Working with an occupational therapist can help individuals adapt their daily routines and environments to reduce fall risk. This might include learning new techniques for moving safely, making home modifications, or using adaptive equipment.

8. Cognitive and Behavioral Strategies:

  - Cognitive Training: Cognitive exercises and brain games can help improve reaction times, decision-making, and overall cognitive function, all of which can contribute to better balance and reduced fall risk.

  - Behavioral Modifications: Encouraging older adults to avoid risky behaviors, take their time when moving, and remain vigilant about their surroundings can significantly reduce the likelihood of falls.

Conclusion

Aging presents numerous challenges, particularly when it comes to maintaining balance and preventing falls. The decline in muscle strength, joint flexibility, and sensory function, along with the impact of health conditions, medications, and environmental factors, all contribute to an increased risk of falls as we age. However, by understanding these challenges and taking proactive steps—such as regular exercise, home modifications, proper footwear, and medication management—older adults can significantly reduce their risk of falls and continue to live safely and independently. Preventing falls is not only about avoiding injuries but also about preserving quality of life and maintaining the confidence to stay active and engaged in daily activities.

Benefits of Balance Exercises

Balance is a fundamental aspect of physical health that allows us to perform everyday activities with ease and safety. However, balance often declines with age, injury, or certain health conditions, leading to an increased risk of falls and a loss of confidence in one's ability to move freely. Incorporating balance exercises into a regular fitness routine can have significant benefits, including improving stability, enhancing mobility, and boosting confidence. This article explores these benefits and highlights why balance exercises are essential for maintaining overall well-being.

Enhancing Stability

1.   Strengthening Core Muscles:

The Core's Role in Balance: The core muscles, which include the abdominal, back, and pelvic muscles, play a crucial role in maintaining balance. These muscles stabilize the spine and pelvis, allowing for controlled movement and preventing falls. Balance exercises, such as planks or stability ball exercises, specifically target the core, improving overall stability.

Improved Posture: Strong core muscles contribute to better posture, which is essential for balance. Good posture keeps the body's center of gravity aligned, reducing the likelihood of falls, particularly when standing or walking on uneven surfaces.

2.   Improving Joint Stability:

Ankle and Hip Strength: The ankles and hips are key joints involved in balance. Strengthening the muscles around these joints through exercises like single-leg stands, heel raises, or lateral leg lifts enhances joint stability. This increased stability helps the body make quick adjustments to maintain balance, especially when faced with sudden changes in terrain or unexpected shifts in weight.

3. Proprioception Enhancement:

Awareness of Body Position: Proprioception is the body's ability to sense its position in space, which is critical for maintaining balance. Balance exercises, such as standing on one leg with eyes closed or using a balance board, challenge and improve proprioception by forcing the body to rely on internal cues rather than visual or external feedback. This heightened sense of body awareness helps prevent falls and enhances overall stability.

Boosting Mobility

1. Increasing Range of Motion:

- Flexibility and Balance: Many balance exercises also improve flexibility, particularly in the joints and muscles that support movement. Exercises like yoga or Tai Chi, which combine balance with gentle stretching, help increase the range of motion in the hips, ankles, and shoulders. This greater flexibility allows for smoother, more fluid movements, making it easier to perform daily activities like bending, reaching, or turning.

- Reduced Stiffness: Regular balance training can reduce stiffness in the muscles and joints, which is a common issue as we age. By keeping the body limber, balance exercises help maintain mobility and prevent the limitations that can come with stiffness and reduced flexibility.

2. Improving Gait and Coordination:

- Steadier Walking Patterns: Balance exercises often focus on improving the coordination between different parts of the body, which is essential for a steady gait. Practicing exercises that involve walking in a straight line, side-stepping, or navigating around obstacles can enhance coordination, leading to a more stable and confident walking pattern.

- Coordination of Movements: Enhanced coordination allows for more precise and controlled movements, reducing the risk of trips and falls. Exercises that require coordinating arm and leg movements, such as marching in place or arm-leg crossovers, help improve overall body coordination, contributing to better mobility.

3. Preventing Mobility Decline:

- Counteracting Age-Related Decline: As people age, there is often a natural decline in mobility due to muscle loss, joint stiffness, and reduced physical activity. Regular balance exercises can slow or even reverse this decline by maintaining muscle strength, joint flexibility, and coordination. This preservation of mobility is key to remaining active and independent in daily life.

Building Confidence

1. Reducing Fear of Falling:

- Overcoming Anxiety: Fear of falling is a common issue, particularly among older adults or those who have previously experienced a fall. This fear can lead to reduced physical activity, which in turn weakens muscles and further impairs balance. By practicing balance exercises and gradually improving stability, individuals can build confidence in their ability to move safely, reducing the anxiety that often accompanies balance issues.

- Increased Self-Efficacy: As balance improves, so does the individual's confidence in their physical abilities. Completing balance exercises and noticing stability improvements can lead to a greater sense of self-efficacy—the belief in one's ability to perform tasks and handle physical challenges. This increased confidence encourages continued participation in physical activities, further enhancing balance and overall health.

2. Encouraging Independence:

- Maintaining Daily Functionality: Improved balance allows individuals to perform daily activities with greater ease and less assistance, whether it's walking up stairs, carrying groceries, or getting in and out of a car. This independence is crucial for maintaining a high quality of life and staying active and engaged in the community.

- Empowering Active Lifestyles: With greater balance and stability, individuals are more likely to participate in recreational activities such as dancing, hiking, or playing sports. This not only contributes to physical health but also supports mental and emotional well-being by enabling social interaction and enjoyment of life's activities.

3. Preventing Injuries and Setbacks:

- Proactive Injury Prevention: By regularly practicing balance exercises, individuals can prevent the injuries that often result from falls. This proactive approach to balance training reduces the likelihood of setbacks that could lead to decreased physical activity and a decline in overall health. Knowing that they are taking steps to protect themselves from injury further boosts confidence in their ability to lead an active and healthy life.

Conclusion

Balance exercises offer a wide range of benefits that go beyond simply preventing falls. By improving stability, enhancing mobility, and boosting confidence, these exercises contribute to overall physical health and well-being. Whether you are an older adult looking to maintain independence, an athlete aiming to enhance performance, or simply someone who wants to stay active and agile, incorporating balance exercises into your routine is a powerful way to support your body and mind. With consistent practice, the gains in balance, strength, and confidence can help you move through life with greater ease, safety, and assurance.

Chapter 2: Preparing for the Program

- Creating a Safe Exercise Environment
    Setting Up at Home
- Warm-Up Essentials
    A Simple Routine to Prepare Your Body

Creating a Safe Environment for Exercise

Before beginning any exercise program, especially one focused on balance, it's essential to ensure that the environment is safe and free from potential hazards. A safe exercise space will minimize the risk of falls and injuries, which is particularly important for seniors who may already be at a higher risk.

Setting Up at Home

Exercising at home offers convenience and comfort, but it also requires careful preparation. Here are several key steps to ensure your home environment is conducive to safe and effective exercise:

1. _Clear the Space_: Choose a space in your home that is free of clutter, furniture, and other objects that could be tripping hazards. A living room or bedroom with an open area is ideal. Ensure that the floor is free of loose rugs or cords, and keep pets in another room to avoid unexpected interruptions.

2. _Stable Surface_: It's important to exercise on a stable, even surface. If you are working on hardwood or tile floors, consider using a non-slip exercise mat to provide cushioning and prevent slips. Avoid exercising on thick carpets, which can be uneven and may hinder balance exercises.

3. _Proper Lighting_: Adequate lighting is crucial to help you see your surroundings clearly and maintain focus. Exercise in a well-lit room to minimize shadows or dim areas that could affect your perception and coordination.

4. _Supportive Furniture_: For certain exercises, having a sturdy chair or countertop nearby for support can help you feel more confident. Make sure the furniture you use is stable and won't move if you lean on it for balance. Avoid using lightweight or unstable chairs, as they can tip over easily.

5. _Accessible Water and Towel_: Keep a bottle of water and a towel nearby. Staying hydrated during exercise is important, especially for seniors, as dehydration can lead to dizziness or muscle cramps. A towel can help with perspiration and keep your hands dry, which is important for maintaining a good grip on any equipment you may be using.

6. _Footwear_: Wear proper footwear that provides good support and traction. Avoid slippers or socks without grips, as these can increase the risk of slipping. If possible, wear athletic shoes with non-slip soles that offer cushioning and stability.

Warm-Up Essentials

Warming up before any physical activity is essential to prepare your body for exercise. A proper warm-up increases blood flow to the muscles improves flexibility, and helps prevent injuries. For seniors, warm-up exercises should be gentle and focused on gradually increasing the heart rate and loosening up stiff joints.

A Simple Body Preparation Regimen

This basic warm-up routine is designed to be easy to follow and effective for preparing the body for balance exercises. It involves low-impact movements that help to improve circulation, flexibility, and range of motion.

1. Marching in Place (2 minutes): Begin by standing with your feet hip-width apart and gently marching in place. Lift your knees as high as is comfortable, and swing your arms in rhythm with your steps. This movement warms up the leg muscles and helps to get your heart rate up.

2. Arm Circles (1 minute): Extend your arms out to the sides at shoulder height. Slowly make small circles with your arms, gradually increasing the size of the circles. After 30 seconds, reverse the direction of the circles. This exercise helps loosen the shoulder joints and warms up the upper body.

3. Ankle Rolls (1 minute): Stand near a wall or chair for support if needed. Lift one foot off the ground and gently roll your ankle in a circular motion. Do this for 30 seconds, then switch to the other foot. Ankle rolls improve flexibility in the ankle joints, which is important for balance and stability.

4. Torso Twists (1 minute): Stand with your feet shoulder-width apart and place your hands on your hips. Slowly twist your torso to the right, allowing your shoulders and head to follow the movement. Return to the center and then twist to the left. Repeat this motion for 1 minute. Torso twists help warm up the core muscles and improve flexibility in the spine.

5. Calf Stretches (1 minute): Stand facing a wall with your hands resting on it for support. Step one foot back and press your heel into the ground while bending your front knee slightly. Hold the stretch for 30 seconds, then switch to the other leg. Calf stretches help prepare the lower legs and ankles for standing and walking exercises.

6. Neck Rolls (1 minute): Sit or stand in a comfortable position. Slowly lower your chin towards your chest and then gently roll your head to one side, bringing your ear towards your shoulder. Continue rolling your head in a slow circle, then reverse direction after 30 seconds. Neck rolls help to release tension in the neck and shoulders, which can often become stiff, particularly for those who spend long periods sitting.

Chapter 3: The 4-Week Balance Program Overview

- Program Structure
  - Daily 10-Minute Routines
  - Tracking Your Progress: Simple Log and Reflection
- Illustrations and How to Follow Them
  - Quick Tips for Using the Visual Guides

This chapter introduces the structure and key components of the 4-week balance program. It provides an overview of the daily routines, the importance of tracking progress, and how to effectively use the illustrations and visual guides to support the exercises. The program is designed to be accessible, effective, and easy to follow, especially for seniors looking to improve their stability and mobility.

Program Structure

The 4-week balance program is built around short, focused exercise sessions that can be completed in just 10 minutes a day. These routines are designed to gradually enhance balance, coordination, and stability. By following the program consistently, you can expect to see improvements in both your physical abilities and overall confidence.

Daily 10-Minute Routines

The core of this program is a series of daily 10-minute exercise routines. Each week focuses on a specific area of balance and stability, with the exercises gradually increasing in difficulty as you progress through the program. The goal is to make these exercises easy to integrate into your daily life, ensuring you can maintain a consistent practice without feeling overwhelmed.

- *Week 1: Building a Foundation* – The first week focuses on basic balance exercises that help strengthen the core and improve postural alignment. The exercises this week are seated and supported, making them accessible to those just starting or those who may have mobility limitations.

- *Week 2: Strengthening Your Balance* – In the second week, the focus shifts to strengthening the lower body, which is crucial for maintaining balance while standing and walking. The exercises include standing movements and light resistance training to build muscle strength and improve coordination.

- *Week 3: Enhancing Mobility and Flexibility* – The third week emphasizes flexibility and coordination. Stretching exercises and mobility drills help increase your range of motion, which is essential for maintaining stability during dynamic movements.

- *Week 4: Advanced Balance and Stability* – The final week introduces more advanced balance exercises, including dynamic movements that challenge your stability in multiple planes. These exercises build on the foundation laid in the previous weeks, helping you achieve greater confidence in your ability to move safely and securely.

Tracking Your Progress: Simple Log and Reflection

Tracking your progress throughout the program is essential for staying motivated and ensuring that you are improving over time. Keeping a simple log of your daily exercises allows you to see how far you've come and identify areas where you may need to focus more attention.

- Daily Exercise Log: Each day, record the exercises you completed, noting any challenges or successes. This log helps you stay accountable and provides a visual record of your efforts.

- Weekly Reflection: At the end of each week, take a few moments to reflect on your progress. How do you feel compared to when you started? Are certain exercises becoming easier? Do you notice improvements in your balance and mobility? These reflections can boost your confidence and help you stay committed to the program.

Illustrations and How to Follow Them

Visual aids are a key component of this program, helping to clarify how each exercise should be performed. The illustrations provided in this book are designed to be easy to follow, showing proper form and technique to ensure you perform each movement safely and effectively.

Quick Tips for Using the Visual Guides

1. Understand the Movements: Before attempting any exercise, take the time to carefully study the corresponding illustration. Pay attention to details such as posture, hand and foot placement, and movement direction. The visual guides are intended to supplement the written instructions and give you a clear idea of what each exercise should look like.

2. Match Your Pace: Follow the pace demonstrated in the illustrations. Many of the exercises involve slow, controlled movements that are crucial for improving balance. Rushing through the exercises can reduce their effectiveness and increase the risk of injury, so take your time and perform each movement mindfully.

3. Adjust as Needed: Everybody is different, and it's okay to modify the exercises to suit your abilities. If an illustration shows a movement that feels too challenging or uncomfortable, adjust it slightly while still focusing on the key principles of balance and stability. For example, if an exercise is demonstrated without support, you can perform it next to a chair or wall for added stability.

4. Use Visual Reminders: If you struggle to remember the correct form for certain exercises, consider placing the illustrations where you exercise, such as on a wall or table nearby. Having these visual reminders within view can help you stay on track and ensure you're performing the exercises correctly.

Chapter 4: Week 1 – Building a Foundation

- Core Strength and Basic Balance
    Seated and Supported Exercises
    Reflection: Progress Check-In

This week is all about laying a strong foundation for balance and stability by focusing on core strength and basic balance exercises. The exercises introduced are designed to be gentle yet effective, making them accessible for seniors of all fitness levels. Seated and supported exercises provide a safe starting point, allowing you to build confidence in your movements while minimizing the risk of falls or injury.

Week 1 Overview

- Goal: Build core strength and basic balance
- Exercise Time: 10 minutes per day
- Focus: Seated and supported exercises that strengthen the core and improve postural alignment

Core Strength and Basic Balance

The core is the body's center of power, and a strong core is crucial for maintaining good posture and stability. During Week 1, the exercises will target the core muscles, including the abdominals, lower back, and hips. Alongside core strengthening, basic balance exercises will be introduced to enhance stability in a controlled and safe environment.

Day 1: Seated Marches

- *Exercise*: Sit on a sturdy chair with your feet flat on the ground. Slowly lift one knee towards your chest, then lower it back down and repeat with the other leg. Continue alternating legs in a slow and controlled march for 1-2 minutes.

- *Benefit*: This exercise helps to engage the core while also improving hip mobility and coordination.

Day 2: Seated Torso Twists

- *Exercise*: Sit tall with your feet flat on the ground and hands crossed over your chest. Slowly rotate your torso to the right, then back to the center, and then to the left. Perform this movement for 1-2 minutes.

- *Benefit*: This exercise engages the core muscles, particularly the obliques, and improves spinal mobility.

Day 3: Seated Leg Lifts

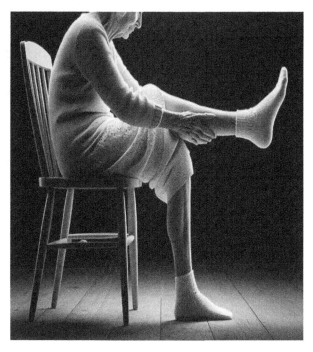

- *Exercise*: Sit on a chair with your back straight and feet flat on the ground. Slowly lift one leg straight out in front of you, hold for a few seconds, and then lower it back down. Alternate legs for 1-2 minutes.

- *Benefit*: Strengthens the quadriceps and engages the core to stabilize your body.

Day 4: Seated Side Leg Lifts

- *Exercise*: Sit upright on a chair with feet flat on the floor. Lift one leg out to the side, keeping it straight, and then return it to the starting position. Repeat with the opposite leg. Perform this movement for 1-2 minutes.

- *Benefit*: Targets the hip abductors, which are important for lateral stability.

Day 5: Seated Heel-to-Toe Rocks

- *Exercise*: Sit in a chair with feet flat on the floor. Slowly lift your heels off the ground, rising onto your toes, then lower your heels and lift your toes. Repeat this rocking motion for 1-2 minutes.

- *Benefit*: Strengthens the calf muscles and improves ankle mobility, both of which are important for maintaining balance while standing and walking.

Day 6: Supported Standing Leg Swings

- *Exercise*: Stand behind a sturdy chair and hold onto the back for support. Gently swing one leg forward and backward in a controlled motion for 1 minute, then switch to the other leg.

- *Benefit*: Engages the hip flexors and glutes while also challenging balance in a supported position.

Day 7: Seated Arm Circles with Light Weights

- *Exercise*: Sit on a chair with your feet flat on the floor and hold light weights (or household items like water bottles) in each hand. Extend your arms out to the sides at shoulder height and perform slow circles for 1 minute. Reverse the direction and continue for another minute.

- *Benefit*: Strengthens the shoulders and upper back while also engaging the core for stability.

Reflection: Progress Check-In

At the end of Week 1, it's important to reflect on your progress. This reflection will help you recognize improvements, identify challenges, and maintain motivation as you move forward in the program.

Questions for Reflection:

1. How do you feel? – Consider how your body feels compared to the beginning of the week. Are the exercises becoming easier to perform? Do you notice any improvements in your posture or overall stability?

2. What challenges did you face? – Reflect on any difficulties you encountered, such as discomfort during certain exercises or trouble maintaining balance. Identifying challenges will help you make adjustments as needed.

3. What are your successes? – Celebrate your accomplishments, no matter how small. Completing the week is a success in itself, and recognizing your progress will help keep you motivated.

4. How is your confidence? – Improving balance is as much about mental confidence as it is about physical ability. Reflect on whether you feel more confident in your ability to move safely and independently.

By taking the time to reflect on your progress, you can set goals for the upcoming weeks and continue to build on the foundation you've established.

Summary

Week 1 is all about building a strong foundation through core-strengthening and basic balance exercises. These seated and supported exercises provide a safe starting point for improving stability and confidence. By the end of the week, you should feel more comfortable with the movements and ready to progress to more challenging exercises in Week 2. The reflection section encourages you to track your progress, recognize your successes, and set goals for continued improvement.

Chapter 5: Week 2 – Strengthening Your Balance

- Lower Body Strength and Balance
    Standing Exercises and Light Resistance
    Reflection: Celebrating Small Wins

Week 2 of the program focuses on strengthening the lower body and enhancing balance through standing exercises and the introduction of light resistance. Building strength in the lower body is crucial for improving balance and stability, particularly as it directly impacts activities such as walking, climbing stairs, and standing from a seated position. This week's exercises are designed to be challenging yet accessible, helping you continue progressing in your balance training journey.

Week 2 Overview

- Goal: Strengthen lower body muscles and improve standing balance
- Exercise Time: 10 minutes per day
- Focus: Standing exercises with light resistance to build muscle strength and stability

<u>*Lower Body Strength and Balance*</u>

Strengthening the lower body is key to maintaining balance and preventing falls. The exercises this week target major muscle groups such as the quadriceps, hamstrings, glutes, and calves. Additionally, these exercises challenge your balance by requiring you to maintain stability in a standing position, sometimes with light resistance to further engage your muscles.

Day 1: Chair Squats

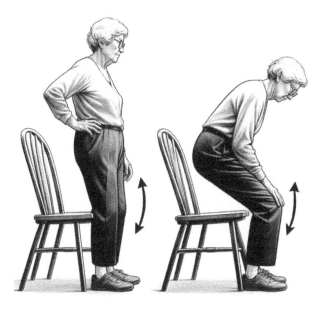

- *Exercise*: Stand in front of a chair with feet hip-width apart. Slowly lower yourself towards the chair as if you are going to sit, but stop just before touching the chair. Hold for a moment, then stand back up. Repeat for 1-2 minutes.

- *Benefit*: Strengthens the quadriceps, glutes, and core muscles while improving balance in a standing position.

Day 2: Heel Raises

- *Exercise*: Stand behind a sturdy chair and hold onto the back for support. Slowly rise onto your toes, lifting your heels off the ground. Hold the position for a few seconds, then lower your heels back down. Repeat for 1-2 minutes.

- *Benefit*: Strengthens the calf muscles and improves balance by challenging the stability on your toes.

Day 3: Side Leg Raises

- *Exercise*: Stand beside a sturdy chair, holding on for support. Slowly lift one leg out to the side, keeping it straight, then lower it back down. Repeat for 1-2 minutes on each side.

- *Benefit*: Strengthens the hip abductors and glutes, which are essential for lateral stability and balance.

Day 4: Standing Marches

- *Exercise*: Stand tall with your feet hip-width apart. Slowly lift one knee towards your chest, then lower it and repeat with the other leg, as if you're marching in place. Continue for 1-2 minutes.

- *Benefit*: Engages the hip flexors, quadriceps, and core muscles while improving coordination and balance.

Day 5: Standing Leg Curls

- *Exercise*: Stand behind a chair for support. Slowly lift one foot towards your glutes by bending your knee, then lower it back down. Alternate legs and repeat for 1-2 minutes.

- *Benefit*: Strengthens the hamstrings and improves balance and coordination in a standing position.

Day 6: Wall Push-Ups

- *Exercise*: Stand facing a wall with your hands placed against it at shoulder height. Step back slightly so your body is at an angle. Slowly bend your elbows to bring your chest closer to the wall, then push back to the starting position. Repeat for 1-2 minutes.

- *Benefit*: Engages the upper body and core while also requiring balance and stability.

Day 7: Light Resistance Band Leg Extensions

- *Exercise*: Use a resistance band looped around the legs just above the knees. Stand beside a chair for support. Slowly extend one leg backward, keeping it straight, and return to the starting position. Repeat on both sides for 1-2 minutes.

- *Benefit*: Adds light resistance to strengthen the glutes, hamstrings, and core, further challenging your balance.

Reflection: Celebrating Small Wins

Reflecting on your progress is crucial to maintaining motivation and recognizing the benefits of your efforts. This week, as you strengthen your lower body and improve your balance, it's important to celebrate the small wins that contribute to your overall progress.

Questions for Reflection:

1. What improvements have you noticed in your balance? – Reflect on any changes you've observed in your stability during everyday activities, such as standing, walking, or transitioning between seated and standing positions.

2. Which exercises felt easier by the end of the week? – Recognize the exercises that have become more manageable as you've built strength and confidence. Celebrate these improvements as evidence of your hard work.

3. How do you feel about using light resistance? – If you introduced light resistance this week, reflect on how it impacted your exercises. Did it make you feel stronger and more capable? Did it positively challenge you?

4. How is your confidence growing? – Balance training isn't just about physical strength; it's also about building mental confidence in your ability to move safely and independently. Reflect on how your confidence has improved since starting the program.

Celebrating these small wins is essential for staying motivated and focused on the bigger picture of improving your balance and stability.

Summary

Week 2 is all about strengthening your lower body and challenging your balance through standing exercises and light resistance. These exercises target the major muscle groups that play a key role in maintaining stability, helping you build the strength needed to stay steady on your feet. By the end of this week, you should feel more confident in your ability to stand, walk, and move safely, with noticeable improvements in your lower body strength and overall balance. The reflection section encourages you to celebrate your progress, keeping you motivated as you continue with the program.

Chapter 6: Week 3 – Enhancing Mobility and Flexibility

- Flexibility and Coordination
    Stretching and Mobility Drills
    Reflection: Building Confidence

Week 3 focuses on enhancing mobility and flexibility, key components of maintaining balance, and coordination, and preventing falls as we age. Flexibility helps improve range of motion, while mobility ensures that our joints move freely through their full range. By working on these aspects, seniors can increase their ability to perform everyday activities more easily and reduce the risk of injury. The exercises introduced this week are designed to improve flexibility, enhance coordination, and further build confidence in movement.

Week 3 Overview

- Goal: Improve flexibility and coordination for better mobility and balance
- Exercise Time: 10 minutes per day
- Focus: Stretching and mobility drills to enhance range of motion and body awareness

Flexibility and Coordination

This week's exercises will focus on stretching major muscle groups and practicing coordination drills to improve overall mobility. The movements are gentle but effective in increasing flexibility and joint range of motion. Coordination drills will also help synchronize movement patterns, which is essential for preventing falls and improving balance.

Day 1: Seated Hamstring Stretch

- *Exercise*: Sit on a chair with one leg extended straight in front of you and the other foot flat on the ground. Slowly reach towards the extended foot, keeping your back straight. Hold for 20-30 seconds, then switch legs.

- *Benefit*: Stretches the hamstrings and lower back, improving flexibility in the back of the legs, which is essential for mobility and preventing injuries.

Day 2: Seated Shoulder and Chest Stretch

- *Exercise*: Sit tall in a chair. Clasp your hands behind your back and gently lift your arms while squeezing your shoulder blades together. Hold for 20-30 seconds.

- *Benefit*: Stretches the shoulders and chest, improving upper body flexibility and posture, which supports balance.

Day 3: Standing Calf Stretch

- *Exercise*: Stand facing a wall, place your hands against the wall, and step one foot back, keeping it flat on the ground. Lean into the wall to stretch the calf of the back leg. Hold for 20-30 seconds, then switch legs.

- *Benefit*: Improves flexibility in the calf muscles and ankles, crucial for walking and maintaining balance on uneven surfaces.

Day 4: Seated Hip Stretch

- *Exercise*: Sit in a chair with your feet flat on the ground. Cross one ankle over the opposite knee, creating a "figure four" shape. Gently press down on the raised knee to stretch the hip. Hold for 20-30 seconds, then switch sides.

- *Benefit*: Stretches the hips, which can become tight and limit mobility, especially in activities like walking or getting up from a chair.

Day 5: Standing Side Bend

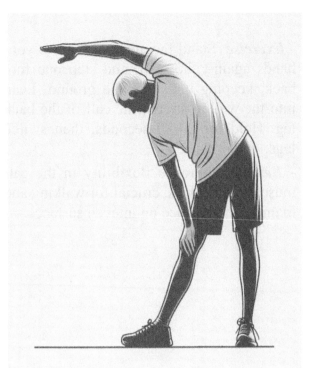

- *Exercise*: Stand with feet shoulder-width apart. Slowly reach one arm overhead and lean to the opposite side, feeling a stretch along the side of your body. Hold for 20-30 seconds, then switch sides.

- *Benefit*: Stretches the sides of the torso and improves flexibility in the spine, helping with mobility and coordination.

Day 6: Seated Ankle Circles

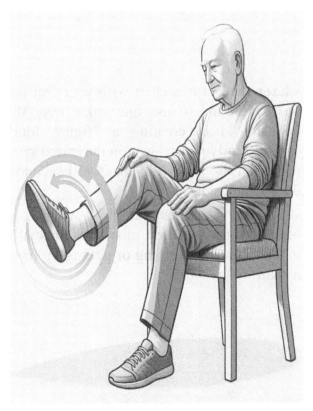

- *Exercise*: Sit in a chair with one leg extended in front of you. Slowly rotate your ankle in a circular motion, first clockwise, then counterclockwise. Repeat for 1 minute, then switch legs.

- *Benefit*: Improves ankle mobility and flexibility, which is essential for maintaining balance during walking and standing.

Day 7: Seated Wrist and Forearm Stretch

- ***Exercise***: Sit tall with one arm extended straight in front of you, palm facing down. Use the opposite hand to gently pull back on your fingers, stretching the wrist and forearm. Hold for 20-30 seconds, then switch sides.

- ***Benefit***: Stretches the wrists and forearms, which can become tight from daily activities. Improving wrist flexibility can aid in overall coordination and upper body movement.

Coordination Drills

In addition to flexibility, coordination drills help synchronize different parts of the body to work together smoothly and effectively. These drills help improve balance by enhancing the body's ability to react to changes in movement or terrain.

Day 1: Seated Ball Pass

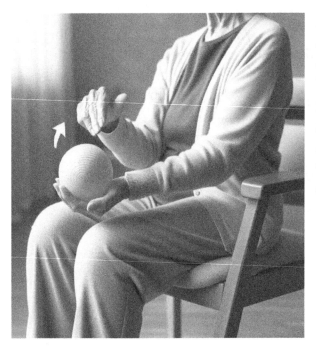

- *Exercise*: Sit on a chair with a small ball or cushion. Pass the ball from one hand to the other in front of your body, then move the ball behind your back and repeat. Continue for 1-2 minutes.

- *Benefit*: Improves hand-eye coordination and core stability while seated, which can translate to better control during daily activities.

Day 2: Standing Heel-to-Toe Walk

- *Exercise*: Stand tall and place one foot directly in front of the other, heel to toe, as if walking on a tightrope. Slowly walk forward, maintaining balance. Repeat for 1-2 minutes.

- *Benefit*: Challenges your balance and coordination, improving your ability to walk steadily and confidently.

Day 3: Seated Foot Taps

- *Exercise*: Sit in a chair with your feet flat on the ground. Lift one foot and tap it gently on the ground in front of you, then return it to the starting position. Alternate feet and continue for 1-2 minutes.

- *Benefit*: Improves coordination between the legs and core, enhancing balance and stability while seated and standing.

Day 4: Standing Arm and Leg Raises

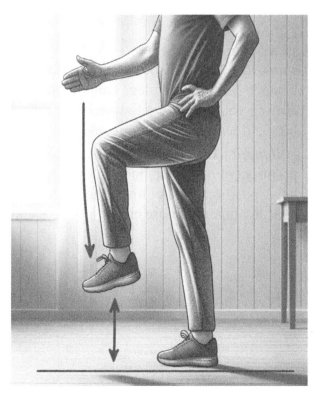

- *Exercise*: Stand tall with feet hip-width apart. Slowly lift one arm and the opposite leg at the same time, then return to the starting position. Repeat on the other side for 1-2 minutes.

- *Benefit*: Enhances coordination between the upper and lower body while also challenging balance and stability.

Day 5: Seated Finger Tapping

- **Exercise**: Sit tall in a chair and extend your arms in front of you. Slowly tap each finger to your thumb, starting with the index finger and moving to the pinky, then reversing the order. Continue for 1-2 minutes.

- **Benefit**: Improves fine motor coordination, which is essential for daily tasks such as buttoning clothes or handling objects.

Day 6: Standing Single-Leg Balance with Eyes Closed

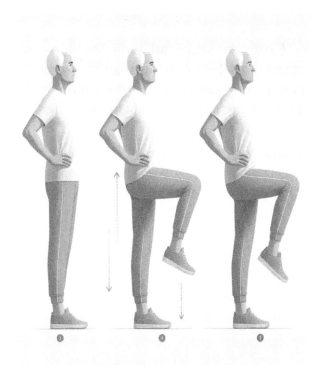

- **Exercise**: Stand next to a chair or wall for support. Lift one foot off the ground and balance on the other leg. Once steady, try closing your eyes for a few seconds. Switch legs and repeat for 1-2 minutes.

- **Benefit**: Challenges your balance and proprioception (your body's awareness of its position), helping to improve coordination in a more challenging context.

Day 7: Seated Ball Toss

- *Exercise*: Sit in a chair with a small ball or cushion. Toss the ball gently into the air and catch it. Continue for 1-2 minutes.

- *Benefit*: Improves hand-eye coordination and focus, which are essential for maintaining balance and avoiding falls.

Reflection: Building Confidence

Week 3 emphasizes the connection between physical movement and confidence. As you enhance your flexibility and coordination, you should feel more capable in your everyday activities. This week's reflection focuses on building mental confidence alongside your physical progress.

Questions for Reflection:

1. How has your mobility improved? – Reflect on how your range of motion has changed. Are you able to move more freely or easily during daily tasks, such as bending, reaching, or turning?

2. How has your coordination improved? – Consider how the coordination drills have impacted your movement. Do you feel more synchronized and in control of your body?

3. What activities feel easier now? – Reflect on specific tasks that have become easier to perform, such as standing up, walking, or reaching for objects. Acknowledge these improvements as confidence boosters.

4. How has your confidence grown? – Balance and mobility training is not just about physical changes; it's about building the confidence to move safely and independently. Reflect on how your mental confidence has grown alongside your physical progress.

Summary

Week 3 focuses on improving flexibility and coordination through stretching and mobility drills. These exercises help increase your range of motion, improve joint flexibility, and enhance your ability to coordinate movements smoothly. By the end of this week, you should notice improvements in your overall mobility and confidence in your ability to move freely and safely. The reflection section encourages you to celebrate these changes, further
reinforcing your commitment to the program and your journey to better balance.

Chapter 7: Week 4 – Advanced Balance and Stability

- Advanced Movements
   Dynamic Balance Exercises
   Reflection: Reviewing Your Progress

Week 4 is the final week of the program and focuses on advanced balance and stability exercises. These exercises incorporate dynamic movements that challenge balance in more complex ways, simulating real-life situations that require coordination, stability, and strength. The goal of this week is to consolidate the progress made in previous weeks, pushing your body and mind to adapt to more challenging movements that further improve your overall balance and stability.

Week 4 Overview

- Goal: Strengthen advanced balance and stability through dynamic exercises
- Exercise Time: 10 minutes per day
- Focus: Dynamic balance exercises that mimic real-life movements

Advanced Movements

This week's exercises are designed to push your balance and stability further by incorporating more dynamic movements. These exercises involve shifting weight, multi-directional movements, and coordination challenges. By practicing these advanced exercises, you'll develop the strength and agility needed to maintain stability in a variety of situations.

Day 1: Single-Leg Stand with Reach

- *Exercise*: Stand tall and lift one foot off the ground, balancing on the other. While balancing, reach one arm forward, then return to the starting position. Repeat for 1-2 minutes on each leg.

- *Benefit*: Improves single-leg balance and coordination while also engaging the core and upper body.

Day 2: Step-Ups

- *Exercise*: Use a step or sturdy platform. Step one foot onto the platform, then bring the other foot up to meet it. Step back down and repeat for 1-2 minutes, alternating the leading leg.

- *Benefit*: Enhances balance and stability in the legs while simulating real-life activities like climbing stairs.

Day 3: Lateral Leg Swings

- *Exercise*: Stand tall and hold onto a chair for support. Swing one leg out to the side, then back across the body in a controlled motion. Repeat for 1-2 minutes on each side.

- *Benefit*: Challenges lateral stability and balance while also strengthening the hips and legs.

Day 4: Clock Reach

- *Exercise*: Imagine you are standing in the center of a clock. Lift one foot slightly off the ground and reach that leg towards the numbers on the clock face (e.g., 12, 3, 6, 9), bringing it back to the center after each reach. Repeat for 1-2 minutes on each leg.

- *Benefit*: Improves balance and proprioception (awareness of your body's position) in multiple directions.

Day 5: Toe Taps

- *Exercise*: Stand in front of a step or low platform. Tap one foot onto the platform, then switch feet, alternating taps for 1-2 minutes.

- *Benefit*: Engages balance and coordination, especially when performed at a faster pace.

Day 6: Heel-to-Toe Walking Backward

- *Exercise*: Walk backward in a straight line, placing the heel of one foot directly behind the toes of the other foot, as if walking on a tightrope. Continue for 1-2 minutes.

- *Benefit*: Enhances coordination and balance while challenging your body's ability to move in reverse.

Day 7: Cross-Step

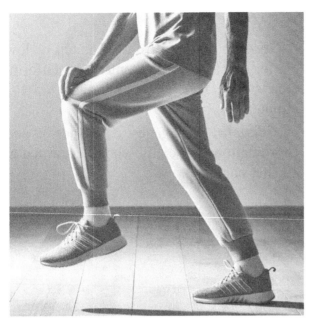

- *Exercise*: Stand tall and take a step diagonally across your body with one foot, then return to the starting position. Repeat on the other side, crossing the opposite leg in front. Continue for 1-2 minutes.

- *Benefit*: Challenges dynamic balance and coordination by incorporating diagonal movement patterns.

Dynamic Balance Exercises

These exercises incorporate movement into balance training, simulating real-life activities that require coordination, agility, and the ability to react to changes in your environment. By practicing dynamic balance, you will improve your ability to stay steady while moving and reduce your risk of falls.

Day 1: Standing Side-to-Side Shifts

- *Exercise*: Stand with feet hip-width apart. Shift your weight to one leg and lift the opposite foot slightly off the ground. Hold for a few seconds, then shift your weight to the other side. Repeat for 1-2 minutes.

- *Benefit*: Enhances your ability to shift weight smoothly from side to side, which is essential for balance during walking and turning.

Day 2: Tandem Walk with Arm Movements

- *Exercise*: Perform a tandem walk (heel-to-toe) while simultaneously moving your arms up and down or side to side. Continue for 1-2 minutes.

- *Benefit*: Engages both upper and lower body coordination, challenging your balance in multiple ways.

Day 3: Single-Leg Balance with Head Turns

- *Exercise*: Stand on one leg and balance. While maintaining your balance, slowly turn your head from side to side. Repeat for 1-2 minutes on each leg.

- *Benefit*: Challenges your balance by introducing head movements, which can simulate real-life scenarios where you need to maintain balance while looking around.

Day 4: Standing Hip Circles

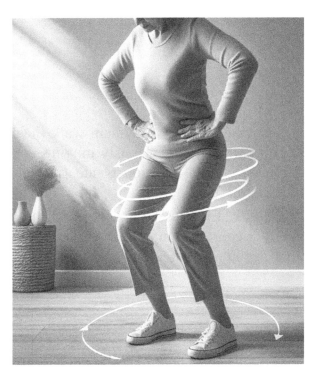

- *Exercise*: Stand with feet hip-width apart. Slowly rotate your hips in a circular motion, first clockwise, then counterclockwise. Repeat for 1-2 minutes.

- *Benefit*: Improves core stability and balance by engaging the hips and lower back in controlled movement.

Day 5: Step and Reach

- *Exercise*: Take a step forward with one foot and simultaneously reach forward with the opposite hand. Return to the starting position and repeat on the other side. Continue for 1-2 minutes.

- *Benefit*: Combines forward movement with upper body coordination, improving balance in a dynamic context.

Day 6: Side Step with Arm Reach

- *Exercise*: Take a large step to the side with one foot while reaching the opposite arm across your body. Return to the starting position and repeat on the other side. Continue for 1-2 minutes.

- *Benefit*: Enhances lateral balance and coordination by combining leg and arm movements in opposite directions.

Day 7: Step Back and Reach Up

- *Exercise*: Take a step back with one foot while reaching both arms up overhead. Return to the starting position and repeat on the other side. Continue for 1-2 minutes.

- *Benefit*: Challenges balance by incorporating backward movement and upper body reach, improving stability and coordination.

Reflection: Reviewing Your Progress

Week 4 is a time to reflect on your entire journey through the balance program. This week's reflection will help you review your progress, celebrate your achievements, and identify areas for continued growth.

Questions for Reflection:

1. How have your balance and stability improved? – Reflect on the changes you've noticed in your balance and stability since starting the program. Are you more confident in your ability to move and stay steady?

2. What challenges did you overcome? – Consider the exercises that were difficult at the beginning but have become easier over time. Acknowledge the effort you put into overcoming these challenges.

3. How do you feel about advanced movements? – Reflect on how your body responded to the advanced exercises this week. Did you feel stronger and more capable? Did the dynamic movements help you feel more prepared for real-life situations?

4. What are your next steps? – Think about how you can continue to build on your progress. What exercises or activities do you want to incorporate into your routine to maintain and improve your balance and stability?

Summary

Week 4 is all about taking your balance and stability training to the next level with advanced movements and dynamic balance exercises. These exercises challenge your body in more complex ways, simulating real-life situations that require coordination, agility, and strength. By the end of this week, you should feel more confident in your ability to maintain balance in a variety of scenarios. The reflection section encourages you to review your progress, celebrate your achievements, and consider your next steps in continuing to improve your balance and stability.

Chapter 8: Post-Program Maintenance Routine

- Maintaining Your Progress

    Daily 10-minute Routine for Ongoing Balance

    Modifying Exercises for Continued Improvement

The goal of this chapter is to help you maintain the balance, stability, and strength you've developed over the 4-week program. Consistency is key to long-term success, and continuing with a daily routine can help you preserve and even improve your progress. This chapter outlines a daily 10-minute routine and provides tips for modifying exercises as you grow stronger and more confident.

Post-Program Overview

- Goal: Maintain and enhance balance, stability, and strength through a consistent daily routine.
- Exercise Time: 10 minutes per day.
- Focus: A balanced routine that includes a mix of exercises for balance, flexibility, and strength.
- Key Element: Modifying exercises to ensure continued improvement.

Maintaining Your Progress

The post-program phase focuses on incorporating what you've learned into your daily life. By continuing with a regular balance routine, you'll help maintain the benefits you've gained, such as improved stability, reduced risk of falls, and enhanced confidence in your mobility. The key is to make this routine a permanent part of your daily life.

Daily 10-Minute Routine for Ongoing Balance

The following routine should be done daily to maintain your balance, strength, and flexibility. The exercises are designed to be simple yet effective, and they can be done at home with minimal equipment.

Exercise 1: Seated Leg Extensions (2 minutes)

- *How to do it*: Sit tall in a chair with feet flat on the floor. Slowly extend one leg out in front of you until it is straight, then lower it back down. Repeat on the other leg.

- *Benefit*: Maintains leg strength, particularly in the quadriceps, which are essential for standing up and walking with stability.

Exercise 2: Standing Heel Raises (2 minutes)

- *How to do it*: Stand with feet hip-width apart and hold onto the back of a chair for support. Slowly rise onto your toes, lifting your heels off the ground. Hold for a second at the top, then lower back down. Repeat.

- *Benefit*: Strengthens the calves and improves ankle stability, which is crucial for balance during walking and standing.

Exercise 3: Seated Ankle Circles (1 minute)

- ***How to do it***: Sit in a chair with one leg extended. Slowly rotate your ankle in a circular motion, first clockwise, then counterclockwise. Repeat with the other leg.

- ***Benefit***: Maintains flexibility and mobility in the ankles, which are vital for adapting to different surfaces and maintaining balance.

Exercise 4: Standing Side Leg Lifts (2 minutes)

- ***How to do it***: Stand tall and hold onto a chair for balance. Slowly lift one leg out to the side, keeping it straight, then lower it back down. Repeat on the other leg.

- ***Benefit***: Strengthens the hips and outer thighs, which are important for lateral stability and balance.

Exercise 5: Seated Shoulder Rolls (1 minute)

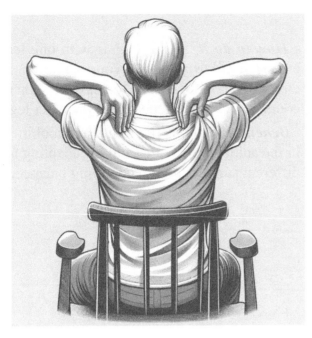

- *How to do it*: Sit in a chair with your back straight. Slowly roll your shoulders up, back, and down in a circular motion. After a minute, reverse the direction.

- *Benefit*: Relieves tension in the shoulders and upper back while promoting good posture, which supports balance.

Exercise 6: Seated Trunk Twists (2 minutes)

- *How to do it*: Sit in a chair with your feet flat on the ground. Place your hands on your knees. Slowly twist your upper body to the right, then return to the center, and twist to the left. Repeat.

- *Benefit*: Improves flexibility and mobility in the spine, which helps with overall movement and balance during daily activities.

Modifying Exercises for Continued Improvement

As you grow stronger and more confident in your balance and mobility, it's important to modify your routine to continue challenging your body. Below are some tips on how to modify exercises to ensure that you're always progressing.

1. Increase Repetitions or Duration

- ***How to modify***: As you feel more comfortable with the exercises, gradually increase the number of repetitions or the amount of time you spend on each movement. For example, if you start with 10 repetitions of an exercise, try increasing to 12 or 15 repetitions as you get stronger.
- ***Benefit***: Increasing the volume of your exercises helps build endurance and strength, ensuring that you continue to see improvements.

2. Reduce Support

- ***How to modify***: If you've been holding onto a chair or wall for balance, try reducing your support by using just one hand or by simply hovering your hands above the chair for added stability.
- ***Benefit***: Reducing your reliance on external support forces your body to work harder to maintain balance, which can help further improve your stability and coordination.

3. Add Light Resistance

- ***How to modify***: Incorporate light resistance into your routine by using resistance bands or light weights. For example, when doing seated leg extensions, you can place a resistance band around your legs to add extra resistance.
- ***Benefit***: Adding resistance challenges your muscles to work harder, which can increase strength and stability.

4. Incorporate Multi-Tasking Movements

- *How to modify*: To further challenge your balance, try incorporating multi-tasking movements into your exercises. For example, when doing standing side leg lifts, you can add an arm movement, such as raising your arms overhead or to the side.
- *Benefit*: Combining upper and lower body movements challenges your coordination and balance, simulating real-life scenarios where you need to perform multiple tasks at once.

5. Try Different Surfaces

- How to modify: To increase the challenge of your balance exercises, try performing them on different surfaces, such as standing on a soft mat or a balance pad.

- Benefit: Practicing balance on unstable surfaces helps improve your body's ability to adapt to changes in terrain, which is essential for preventing falls in real-life situations.

Reflection: Long-Term Progress

In this post-program phase, it's essential to reflect on your long-term progress. The key is to stay consistent with your routine and continue challenging yourself with modifications. Celebrate your achievements so far and set new goals for maintaining and improving your balance, stability, and mobility.

Questions for Reflection:

1. How consistent have you been with your routine? – Reflect on how often you've been doing your exercises and what has helped you stay consistent.

2. What improvements have you noticed? – Consider how your balance, strength, and flexibility have changed since completing the 4-week program.

3. How can you continue to challenge yourself? – Think about what modifications or new exercises you can incorporate into your routine to keep progressing.

4. What are your long-term goals? – Set new goals for maintaining your progress and continuing to improve your balance and stability.

Summary

The post-program maintenance routine is all about maintaining and enhancing the progress you've made. By committing to a daily 10-minute routine and gradually modifying your exercises, you'll be able to maintain your balance, strength, and flexibility for the long term. The key is to stay consistent, challenge yourself, and continue reflecting on your progress to ensure that you're always moving forward in your journey to better balance and stability.

Chapter 9: Lifestyle Tips for Better Balance

- Healthy Habits
    Nutrition and Hydration Tips
- Mind-Body Connection
    Relaxation and Mindfulness Techniques

Healthy Habits

Nutrition and Hydration Tips

Balance is a vital aspect of physical health, especially as we age. While exercise and physical activity are key to maintaining good balance, nutrition and hydration also play crucial roles. A well-balanced diet and proper hydration can enhance muscle function, support joint health, and improve overall bodily function, all of which contribute to better balance. This chapter will explore the importance of nutrition and hydration for balance, offering practical tips to incorporate these elements into daily life.

The Role of Nutrition in Balance

1.   **Muscle Strength and Maintenance**:

Protein Intake: Muscles are the primary stabilizers of the body, and maintaining muscle strength is essential for good balance. Protein is a critical nutrient for muscle repair and growth. Consuming adequate amounts of protein from sources such as lean meats, fish, eggs, dairy products, beans, and legumes can help preserve muscle mass, especially as we age.

Amino Acids: Essential amino acids, the building blocks of protein, play a direct role in muscle synthesis. Including a variety of protein sources ensures the body receives all the essential amino acids it needs to maintain muscle strength and support balance.

2.   **Bone Health**:

Calcium and Vitamin D: Strong bones provide the framework for the body, contributing to overall stability. Calcium is vital for bone health, and it is best absorbed when paired with vitamin D. Dairy products, leafy green vegetables, fortified cereals, and fish like salmon are excellent sources of calcium. Vitamin D can be obtained from sunlight exposure, fortified foods, and supplements if necessary.

Magnesium and Phosphorus: These minerals are also important for bone health. Magnesium, found in nuts, seeds, whole grains, and leafy greens, helps with calcium absorption, while phosphorus, available in meat, dairy, and legumes, works alongside calcium to build strong bones

3.   **Joint Health**:

Anti-Inflammatory Foods: Inflammation in the joints can lead to stiffness and pain, which can impair balance. Anti-inflammatory foods, such as omega-3 fatty acids found in fish, flaxseeds, and walnuts, can help reduce joint inflammation. Additionally, antioxidants from fruits and vegetables, particularly those rich in vitamins C and E, can protect joints by neutralizing free radicals that cause damage.

Collagen and Gelatin: Collagen, a protein found in the connective tissues of the body, supports joint health. Bone broth, gelatin, and collagen supplements can help maintain joint flexibility and reduce the risk of balance issues related to joint problems.

4.   **Nervous System Support**:

B Vitamins: The nervous system plays a critical role in balance by coordinating muscle movements and sensory feedback. B vitamins, particularly B12, B6, and folate, are essential for nervous system function. These vitamins are found in a variety of foods, including whole grains, eggs, fish, poultry, and leafy greens. Ensuring adequate intake of these vitamins supports the nervous system's role in maintaining balance.

Healthy Fats: Omega-3 fatty acids, in addition to their anti-inflammatory properties, support brain health and nerve function. Including sources like fatty fish, flaxseeds, and walnuts in the diet can improve communication between the brain and muscles, enhancing balance.

Hydration and Balance

1.   **Importance of Hydration**:

Maintaining Muscle and Joint Function: Adequate hydration is essential for maintaining muscle function and joint lubrication. Dehydration can lead to muscle cramps, stiffness, and decreased joint flexibility, all of which can impair balance. Water is crucial for transporting nutrients to muscles and joints, aiding in their function and recovery.

Preventing Dizziness and Confusion: Dehydration can also affect cognitive function, leading to dizziness, lightheadedness, and confusion—all of which increase the risk of falls. Staying well-hydrated helps maintain mental clarity and reduces the likelihood of balance-related issues.

2. **Daily Hydration Tips**:

Set Hydration Goals: Aim to drink at least 8-10 cups (2-2.5 liters) of water per day, adjusting based on activity level, climate, and individual needs. Carrying a water bottle throughout the day can serve as a reminder to stay hydrated.

Incorporate Hydrating Foods: In addition to drinking water, consuming foods with high water content, such as cucumbers, watermelon, oranges, and leafy greens, can contribute to overall hydration.

Monitor Hydration Levels: Pay attention to signs of dehydration, such as dark urine, dry mouth, or feeling unusually tired. Monitoring urine color is a simple way to assess hydration; it should be light yellow or clear.

3. **Electrolyte Balance**:

Importance of Electrolytes: Electrolytes, such as sodium, potassium, and magnesium, are minerals that help regulate fluid balance, muscle contractions, and nerve signals. An imbalance in electrolytes can lead to muscle weakness, cramps, and dizziness, all of which can impair balance.

Sources of Electrolytes: Incorporate foods rich in electrolytes, such as bananas, avocados, nuts, seeds, and yogurt, into your diet. During periods of intense physical activity or hot weather, consider drinking electrolyte-rich beverages to replenish lost minerals.

Practical Tips for Incorporating Nutrition and Hydration into Daily Life

1. **Balanced Meals**:

Focus on Variety: Aim to include a variety of nutrient-rich foods in each meal to ensure you're getting a balanced intake of proteins, healthy fats, vitamins, and minerals. A balanced diet supports all aspects of health, including balance.

Plan Ahead: Meal planning can help ensure that your diet includes all the necessary nutrients to support balance. Consider preparing meals in advance or keeping healthy snacks on hand to avoid nutrient gaps.

2.   **Mindful Eating**:

Listen to Your Body: Pay attention to your body's hunger and thirst cues. Eating and drinking when you're genuinely hungry or thirsty, rather than out of habit, can help ensure that your nutritional and hydration needs are met.

Moderation and Portion Control: Eating in moderation and controlling portion sizes can help maintain a healthy weight, which is important for balance. Excess weight can strain the joints and muscles, leading to balance issues.

3.   **Supplementation**:

o   **When Necessary**: In some cases, supplements may be necessary to fill nutritional gaps, especially for older adults or those with specific dietary restrictions. Consult with a healthcare provider to determine if supplements like calcium, vitamin D, or omega-3 fatty acids are appropriate for you.

Quality Matters: If you choose to take supplements, opt for high-quality products that are tested for purity and efficacy. This ensures you're getting the intended benefits without unnecessary additives.

4.   **Hydration Routine**:

Start the Day with Water: Begin each day with a glass of water to kickstart hydration. This habit can set a positive tone for staying hydrated throughout the day.

Set Reminders: Use alarms or apps to remind yourself to drink water regularly, especially if you tend to forget or become busy. Regular hydration breaks can become a natural part of your daily routine.

Conclusion

Good balance is integral to maintaining an active, independent lifestyle, and nutrition and hydration play significant roles in supporting this aspect of health. By focusing on a diet rich in proteins, vitamins, minerals, and healthy fats, and by ensuring adequate hydration, you can enhance muscle function, support joint and bone health, and keep the nervous system functioning optimally. These dietary practices, combined with regular physical activity, will help maintain and even improve balance, reducing the risk of falls and boosting confidence in your ability to move safely through daily life.

Mind-Body Connection

The mind-body connection plays a significant role in maintaining balance and preventing falls. By practicing relaxation and mindfulness techniques, you can reduce stress, improve focus, and enhance your body's awareness of its position in space. This can help you react more effectively to changes in your environment and prevent falls before they happen.

Relaxation Techniques

1. <u>Deep Breathing</u>: Practicing deep breathing exercises can help calm your mind and reduce stress, which can have a positive effect on your balance. When you're stressed, your muscles can tense up, making it harder to maintain stability. Deep breathing promotes relaxation, helping you move with more ease and confidence.

 - *How to Practice*: Sit or lie down in a comfortable position. Close your eyes and take a slow, deep breath through your nose, filling your lungs completely. Hold for a moment, then slowly exhale through your mouth. Repeat for 5-10 minutes to achieve a state of relaxation.

2. <u>Progressive Muscle Relaxation</u>: This technique involves tensing and then relaxing each muscle group in your body, which helps release tension and improve your awareness of how your body feels.

- How to Practice: Starting with your feet, tense your muscles for a few seconds, then release and focus on the feeling of relaxation. Move up your body, tensing and relaxing each muscle group (e.g., legs, abdomen, arms, shoulders, and face). This helps reduce overall tension and improve body awareness.

3. Visualization: Visualization exercises involve imagining yourself in a calm, peaceful environment. This can help reduce anxiety, which is often linked to poor balance and stability.

- How to Practice: Find a quiet space, close your eyes, and visualize yourself in a relaxing setting, such as a beach or a forest. Focus on the sights, sounds, and sensations of the environment. This practice can help calm your mind and promote relaxation, making it easier to maintain your balance in real-life situations.

Mindfulness Techniques

1. Mindful Movement: Paying attention to how your body moves can help you become more aware of your balance and posture. Mindful movement practices, such as Tai Chi and yoga, encourage slow, controlled movements that improve your balance, coordination, and body awareness.

- Tai Chi: This ancient Chinese practice involves slow, flowing movements that enhance balance, flexibility, and strength. Tai Chi emphasizes mindfulness and awareness of your body's position in space, making it an excellent practice for improving balance.
- Yoga: Yoga combines physical postures with breathing exercises and mindfulness. Poses that focus on balance, such as the tree pose, can help improve stability and coordination. Yoga also promotes relaxation and flexibility, both of which support better balance.

2. Body Scan Meditation: This mindfulness practice involves mentally scanning your body from head to toe, paying attention to any areas of tension or discomfort. This helps improve your awareness of how your body feels and can help you adjust your posture and movement to maintain better balance.

- How to Practice: Lie down in a comfortable position and close your eyes. Starting with your head, mentally scan your body, noting any areas of tension or discomfort. As you move down your body, consciously relax each area, letting go of any tightness or stress. This practice can improve your overall body awareness and help you move more mindfully throughout the day.

3. Mindful Walking: This practice involves walking slowly and paying attention to each step you take. By focusing on the sensation of your feet touching the ground, the movement

of your legs, and the rhythm of your breath, you can improve your balance and coordination.

*- **How to Practice***: Find a quiet place where you can walk undisturbed. Begin walking slowly, paying attention to each step. Notice how your feet make contact with the ground and how your body shifts as you move. This practice can help you become more aware of your balance and improve your ability to move with stability.

Reflection: Building Confidence Through Healthy Habits

Incorporating healthy habits and mindfulness techniques into your daily routine can significantly impact your balance and overall well-being. By paying attention to your nutrition, hydration, and mental health, you can enhance your physical capabilities and build confidence in your ability to move safely and steadily.

Questions for Reflection:

1. How can you improve your daily habits? – Reflect on your current diet, hydration, and mindfulness practices. Are there areas where you can make improvements to support better balance and stability?

2. What mindfulness practices work best for you? – Consider which relaxation and mindfulness techniques resonate with you. How can you incorporate them into your daily routine to promote a stronger mind-body connection?

3. How do you feel about your progress so far? – Reflect on how your balance, strength, and mental clarity have improved since adopting healthier habits. What positive changes have you noticed in your overall well-being?

Summary

In Chapter 9, we explore the lifestyle factors that influence balance and stability. By adopting healthy habits, such as proper nutrition and hydration, and practicing mindfulness techniques that strengthen the mind-body connection, you can enhance your balance and reduce the risk of falls. This holistic approach to balance training promotes overall well-being and empowers you to move confidently and safely in your daily life.

Conclusion

- Your Journey to Better Balance
    Encouragement to Continue Your Practice
- Resources
    Printable Logs, Links, and Additional Support

Congratulations on completing this journey to better balance! You've taken an important step toward enhancing your stability, mobility, and confidence. As we conclude this guide, it's important to reflect on your progress, celebrate your achievements, and set the stage for continued success. This chapter will encourage you to keep up your practice, as well as valuable resources to support your ongoing journey.

Your Journey to Better Balance

The path to improving balance and preventing falls is not a one-time effort; it is an ongoing commitment to your health and well-being. Throughout this program, you've built a strong foundation of balance exercises, learned how to strengthen your muscles and joints, and developed techniques to enhance your flexibility and coordination. These are skills that will serve you well in everyday life, helping you move with greater confidence and reducing your risk of falls.

Reflecting on Your Achievements

Take a moment to reflect on the progress you've made. Whether you've noticed improvements in your ability to stand on one leg, increased your flexibility, or simply feel more confident in your movements, every step forward is a victory. Progress can be gradual, and it's important to celebrate even the small wins along the way.

- Physical Progress: Consider the changes in your strength, balance, and flexibility. Have you noticed it's easier to walk, stand, or perform daily activities? These physical improvements are a testament to your hard work.
- Mental Progress: Beyond the physical, think about how your mindset has evolved. Do you feel more confident in your ability to prevent falls and stay active? This mental shift is just as important as your physical progress.

By acknowledging how far you've come, you can stay motivated to continue your balance practice and build on your success.

Encouragement to Continue Your Practice

While you've completed the structured 4-week program, maintaining your balance and mobility requires ongoing practice. The good news is that the habits you've developed during this program are now part of your routine, and continuing them doesn't have to be overwhelming. Consistency is key—by dedicating just 10 minutes a day to balance exercises, you can maintain and even improve the progress you've made.

Here are some tips for continuing your practice:

1. Set New Goals: Now that you've completed the initial program, think about setting new goals to challenge yourself. Whether it's increasing the difficulty of your exercises, extending your practice time, or incorporating more advanced movements, new goals can keep you motivated and focused

2. Stay Consistent: Consistency is crucial for long-term success. Even if you only have a few minutes a day, make it a priority to practice your balance exercises regularly. The more consistent you are, the more likely you are to maintain your progress.

3. Incorporate Balance into Daily Activities: You don't have to limit your balance practice to designated exercise time. Look for opportunities to integrate balance exercises into your daily life. For example, practice standing on one leg while brushing your teeth, or do heel raises while waiting in line.

4. Be Patient with Yourself: Balance training is a journey, and progress can take time. Be patient with yourself and remember that every effort counts. Even on days when you don't feel your best, a little practice is better than none.

Staying Positive and Motivated

It's natural to experience ups and downs in your journey to better balance. Some days you might feel strong and steady, while others may present more challenges. During difficult moments, remind yourself of why you started this journey. Whether your goal is to reduce your risk of falls, regain confidence, or simply stay active as you age, keeping your "why" in mind can help you stay motivated.

Surround yourself with positive influences, such as supportive friends, family members, or a community of like-minded individuals who share your commitment to health and balance. Celebrating your progress with others can make the journey even more rewarding.

Resources

As you continue your journey to better balance, having access to additional resources can provide support and encouragement. This section offers a variety of tools, including printable logs, helpful links, and additional support options to help you stay on track.

Printable Logs

Keeping track of your progress is a great way to stay motivated and see how far you've come. Below are some printable logs you can use to document your balance practice, track your progress, and set new goals.

- Daily Exercise Log: Use this log to record your daily exercises, including the type of exercise, duration, and any modifications you've made. This can help you stay consistent and track your improvements over time.

- Progress Reflection Journal: This journal allows you to reflect on your progress, celebrate your successes, and identify areas for improvement. You can use it to set weekly or monthly goals and track your achievements.

- Balance Challenge Tracker: If you're looking to challenge yourself with new exercises or longer practice times, this tracker can help you stay accountable. Set a challenge (e.g., "stand on one leg for 60 seconds") and record your progress toward achieving it. These logs can serve as a visual reminder of your dedication and progress, helping you stay motivated on your journey to better balance.

Links to Additional Resources

To continue learning and improving your balance, consider exploring these online resources:

- Exercise Videos: Many websites offer free instructional videos on balance exercises, strength training, and flexibility. These can serve as a great supplement to your daily routine and provide new ideas for challenging yourself.

- Balance and Fall Prevention Programs: Some organizations offer specialized programs for seniors that focus on balance and fall prevention. Check with local senior centers, fitness centers, or online platforms to find a program that works for you.

- Support Communities: Joining a community of like-minded individuals can provide motivation, accountability, and support. Look for online forums, social media groups, or in-person classes where you can connect with others who share your goals.

Additional Support

If you feel you need more personalized guidance, consider reaching out to professionals who can offer additional support:

- Physical Therapists: A physical therapist can assess your specific needs and create a personalized balance training program for you. They can also help you modify exercises to suit your abilities and prevent injury.

- Fitness Trainers: A fitness trainer with experience in working with seniors can guide you through exercises that improve balance, strength, and flexibility. They can also help you set new goals and stay on track.

- Healthcare Providers: If you have any concerns about your balance or overall health, don't hesitate to consult your healthcare provider. They can offer advice, refer you to specialists, or recommend additional resources for fall prevention.

Summary

Your journey to better balance doesn't end here—it's a lifelong commitment to staying active, strong, and confident. By continuing your practice, setting new goals, and utilizing the resources available to you, you can maintain and even improve the progress you've made. Remember to celebrate your achievements, stay patient with yourself, and embrace the positive changes that come with regular balance training.

As you move forward, know that you're not alone in this journey. Support is available, whether through online resources, professional guidance, or community connections. Keep striving for better balance, and enjoy the many benefits that come with it: greater mobility, enhanced confidence, and a healthier, more active life.

Appendices

- Safety Tips and FAQs
    Consultation and Prevention Tips
- Exercise Modifications
    Adapting to Different Fitness Levels

As you continue your journey toward better balance and mobility, it's important to prioritize safety, adapt exercises to your fitness level, and address common concerns. The appendices provide practical guidance on staying safe during your balance training, answers to frequently asked questions, and tips on how to modify exercises to suit your abilities.

Safety Tips and FAQs

Consultation and Prevention Tips

Before embarking on any exercise program, especially if you're new to fitness or have any medical conditions, it's essential to consult with a healthcare professional. This ensures that you're physically ready for the exercises and helps prevent injury. Here are some key consultation and prevention tips:

1. Consult with Your Doctor: If you have any pre-existing medical conditions, injuries, or concerns about your health, talk to your doctor before starting this program. They can advise you on any limitations or modifications you may need to make.

2. Get a Balance Assessment: Consider getting a professional balance assessment from a physical therapist or healthcare provider. This can help identify any specific areas of concern, such as muscle imbalances or joint issues, and guide you in choosing the right exercises.

3. Start Slow and Gradual: When starting a new exercise program, it's important to begin at a comfortable pace and gradually increase the intensity. Avoid pushing yourself too hard, especially if you're new to balance exercises.

4. Create a Safe Environment: Ensure that your exercise space is free of clutter, slippery surfaces, or obstacles that could lead to a fall. Use a sturdy chair or wall for support when needed, and consider placing a non-slip mat on the floor to prevent accidents.

5. Stay Hydrated and Rested: Proper hydration and rest are essential for any exercise routine. Drink plenty of water before, during, and after your workout, and ensure you're getting enough sleep to help your body recover.

6. Listen to Your Body: Pay attention to how your body feels during and after exercise. If you experience any pain, dizziness, or discomfort, stop the exercise and consult a

healthcare professional. It's important to differentiate between discomfort from exertion and actual pain.

7. Use Proper Footwear: Wear comfortable, supportive shoes with non-slip soles during your exercises. This helps provide stability and reduces the risk of slipping or twisting your ankle.

8. Stay Consistent but Rest When Needed: Consistency is key to progress, but so is knowing when to rest. If you feel fatigued or sore, take a day off to recover. Overtraining can lead to injury, so it's important to balance exercise with rest.

Frequently Asked Questions (FAQs)

Q: How often should I practice these balance exercises?

A: Consistency is key. Aim to practice the balance exercises daily for 10 minutes as outlined in this program. If daily practice is not possible, try to exercise at least 3-4 times a week.

Q: What should I do if I feel pain during the exercises?

A: Stop the exercise immediately and assess the situation. If the pain persists, consult with your healthcare provider before continuing. It's important to differentiate between discomfort from exertion and actual pain, which could indicate an injury.

Q: Can I do these exercises if I have joint problems or arthritis?

A: Yes, balance exercises can be beneficial for those with joint problems or arthritis, but modifications may be necessary. Consult with your healthcare provider for personalized advice, and start with gentle, low-impact movements.

Q: How do I know if I'm making progress?

A: Progress can be measured in various ways, such as improved stability, reduced fear of falling, increased confidence in daily activities, or the ability to perform exercises with less support. Tracking your progress in a log or journal can also help you see improvements over time.

Q: Are these exercises safe to do alone, or should I have someone with me?

A: While many of the exercises in this program are designed to be done safely at home, it's always a good idea to have someone nearby, especially if you're at risk of falling. If you're unsure, start with exercises that provide ample support and gradually build your confidence.

Q: What should I do if I miss a few days of exercise?

A: Don't worry! Life happens, and missing a few days of exercise is normal. The key is to get back on track when you can. Simply pick up where you left off and continue with the program.

Exercise Modifications

Adapting exercises to suit different fitness levels is crucial for ensuring that the program is accessible and effective for everyone. Whether you're a beginner or more advanced, the following modifications can help you tailor the exercises to your needs.

Adapting for Beginners

If you're new to balance exercises or have limited mobility, start with these beginner-friendly modifications:

1. Seated Exercises: Many balance exercises can be performed while seated in a sturdy chair. This reduces the risk of falling while still allowing you to engage your core and improve stability. For example, practice seated leg lifts or seated marches to build strength in your lower body.

2. Use Support: When standing exercises are required, use a chair, countertop, or wall for support. This provides extra stability and helps build confidence as you progress. Gradually reduce your reliance on support as you become more comfortable.

3. Shorter Duration: If 10 minutes feels too long at first, start with shorter sessions (e.g., 5 minutes) and gradually increase the time as your stamina improves.

4. Slow and Controlled Movements: Focus on performing each exercise slowly and with control. This reduces the risk of injury and allows you to concentrate on maintaining good form.

Modifications for Intermediate and Advanced Levels

For those who are more experienced with balance exercises and want to challenge themselves, consider these modifications:

1. Incorporate Light Resistance: Adding light resistance, such as resistance bands or small hand weights, can increase the intensity of your exercises. For example, use resistance bands during leg lifts or add hand weights during standing balance exercises to engage more muscles.

2. Increase Duration or Repetitions: As your strength and endurance improve, challenge yourself by increasing the duration of your exercises or performing additional repetitions. For example, extend your practice time from 10 minutes to 15 or 20 minutes, or add an extra set of exercises.

3. Challenge Your Stability: To make exercises more challenging, try reducing your base of support. For example, practice standing on one leg without holding onto a support or perform exercises on an uneven surface, such as a balance pad.

4. Dynamic Movements: Advanced practitioners can incorporate dynamic movements that challenge both balance and coordination. For example, practice stepping exercises, such as stepping onto a low platform and back down, or incorporate gentle jumps to engage your muscles more dynamically.

Modifications for Limited Mobility

If you have limited mobility due to injury or a chronic condition, it's important to modify exercises to ensure they remain safe and effective:

1. Gentle Range of Motion: Focus on exercises that promote a gentle range of motion without causing strain or discomfort. For example, practice seated heel raises or gentle seated twists to maintain flexibility and joint mobility.

2. Slow Transitions: If moving between seated and standing positions is difficult, focus on exercises that don't require frequent transitions. You can still work on balance and strength while remaining in one position.

3. Partner Support: If needed, perform exercises with the assistance of a partner or caregiver. They can provide extra stability and ensure your safety throughout the practice.

Summary

The appendices offer vital safety tips, FAQs, and exercise modifications that cater to various fitness levels and abilities. By following the safety guidelines, consulting with healthcare professionals, and using the appropriate exercise modifications, you can tailor your balance training to your needs and progress confidently. Whether you're a beginner or more advanced, remember that balance training is a journey, and making adjustments to your routine will help you continue improving while staying safe and injury-free.

Use the FAQs and printable logs to stay informed and motivated as you maintain your progress, and don't hesitate to adapt exercises as needed. Balance exercises are not one-size-fits-all, and by customizing the program to your abilities, you're setting yourself up for long-term success.

About the Author

Hello! I'm Sarah Lockman, and I'm so excited to guide you through *Balance Exercises for Seniors: 10-Minute Daily Exercises to Improve Stability and Prevent Falls | A 4-Week Illustrated Fitness Guide to Gain Confidence and Mobility at Home.

For over 15 years, I've been immersed in the world of fitness and physical therapy, focusing on the unique needs of seniors. My journey started with a degree from University, and it has since evolved into a passion for helping older adults stay active, balanced, and independent. I've worked in various settings, including community health centers, senior living facilities, and private practices, which has given me a deep understanding of the challenges and opportunities in senior fitness.

What drives me is seeing how transformative a well-designed exercise program can be. Throughout my career, I've witnessed countless individuals gain strength, confidence, and improved mobility from consistent exercise. My approach is to make fitness accessible and enjoyable, with a focus on practical solutions that fit into your daily life. This book is designed to be a friendly, easy-to-follow guide that you can use right at home, no matter your starting point.

In addition to my hands-on experience, I hold certifications in [relevant certifications, e.g., senior fitness, fall prevention, or rehabilitation]. These qualifications have equipped me with the tools and knowledge to create effective programs that cater specifically to the needs of older adults. I'm dedicated to providing clear, actionable advice and exercises that help you build a solid foundation for better balance and overall health.

Thank you for allowing me to be a part of your journey toward better balance and well-being. I'm here to support you every step of the way, and I hope this book empowers you to achieve your fitness goals with confidence and enthusiasm. If you have any questions or need further support, feel free to reach out. Here's to your health and happiness!

Editorial Review

"Balance Exercises for Seniors: 10-Minute Daily Exercises to Improve Stability and Prevent Falls | A 4-Week Illustrated Fitness Guide to Gain Confidence and Mobility at Home" is a standout resource for older adults aiming to boost their balance, stability, and overall well-being. Authored by Sarah Lockman, a respected expert in senior fitness and physical therapy, this book delivers a comprehensive, practical approach to enhancing physical health through targeted exercise routines.

The book's structure is meticulously designed to cater to seniors at various fitness levels, making it an invaluable tool for anyone looking to improve their balance. Over four weeks, readers are guided through daily 10-minute routines that are both manageable and effective. Each exercise is presented with detailed illustrations and step-by-step instructions, ensuring clarity and safety in execution. Sarah Lockman's approach emphasizes gradual progression, starting with foundational exercises and advancing to more complex movements. This incremental approach helps readers build confidence and competence, reducing the risk of injury and maximizing the benefits of each exercise.

One of the key strengths of this guide is its focus on creating a supportive and safe exercise environment. The book offers practical advice on how to set up a home workout space, including tips for minimizing hazards and selecting appropriate equipment. Additionally, it provides essential warm-up routines that prepare the body for exercise, enhancing effectiveness and reducing the risk of strain.

Sarah Lockman brings a wealth of experience to this book, drawing on her extensive background in physical therapy and senior fitness. With certifications, it offers a well-rounded perspective on the challenges and opportunities in senior exercise. This expertise is reflected in the book's thoughtful design and the effectiveness of the exercises.

The guide also includes valuable resources for tracking progress and reflecting on achievements. Simple logs and reflection prompts encourage readers to monitor their improvements and celebrate milestones, fostering a positive and motivating experience. This book aspect helps maintain engagement and commitment throughout the program.

In addition to the exercise routines, "Balance Exercises for Seniors" provides insightful lifestyle tips, including guidance on nutrition, hydration, and mindfulness. These recommendations support a holistic approach to health, emphasizing the interconnectedness of physical, mental, and emotional well-being. Sarah Lockman's focus on the mind-body connection underscores the importance of a balanced lifestyle in achieving and maintaining fitness goals.

Overall, "Balance Exercises for Seniors" is a highly recommended guide for anyone seeking to enhance their balance and prevent falls. It combines Sarah Lockman's deep expertise with a user-friendly approach, making it accessible and effective for older adults. Whether you are just beginning your fitness journey or looking to refine your routine, this book offers the tools, encouragement, and support needed to achieve lasting improvements in balance, mobility, and overall health. Sarah Lockman's dedication to senior fitness shines through in this exceptional guide, making it a valuable addition to any wellness library.

Made in the USA
Las Vegas, NV
07 October 2024

96409649R00057